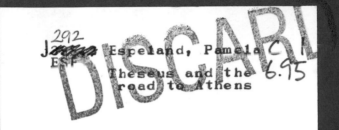
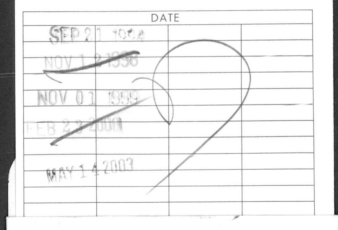

THESEUS
AND THE ROAD TO ATHENS

Pamela Espeland

pictures by Reg Sandland

 Carolrhoda Books, Inc. Minneapolis

to David Porter, who loves what he teaches

LIBRARY OF CONGRESS CATALOGING IN PUBLICATION DATA

Espeland, Pamela, 1951-
Theseus and the road to Athens.

(A Myth for modern children)
SUMMARY: When the time comes for him to join his
father, King Aegeus, in Athens, Theseus decides to walk
in order to test his courage.

1. Theseus—Juvenile literature. [1. Theseus. 2. Mythology,
Greek] I. Sandland, Reg. II. Title.

BL820.T5E84   398.2′2′0938   80-27713
ISBN 0-87614-141-6

2 3 4 5 6 7 8 9 10 92 91 90 89 88 87 86 85 84 83 82

ABOUT THIS STORY

Ancient Greece wasn't very big, but it was very important. All together, the Greek states made up an area about the size of Austria. From this tiny part of the world came many famous people and ideas.

The ancient Greek people were a lot like us. Over 2,000 years ago, their children played and went to school and watched the Olympic games. Grown-ups worked. They wrote plays and poems. They made laws. Their government was the beginning of Western democracy.

But the Greeks didn't know as much as we do about science. So they used myths to explain nature. When there was a storm at sea, they said, "Poseidon, the God of the Sea, must be angry!" When there was a good harvest, they said, "Demeter, the Goddess of the Earth, must be happy!" Not almyths explained nature, though. Some told about Greek history. And some were just good stories.

The Greek civilization lasted for a long time, but it could not last forever. Around 150 B.C., the Romans took it over. They also adopted the Greek gods and goddesses—they just changed their names to Roman names. Most Romans didn't really believe in the gods, but they did like to tell good stories. So they kept on telling the myths.

Theseus was one of the Greeks' favorite heroes. He had many adventures during his life and was always in the middle of something exciting. Because he was so popular, many different writers wrote about him, both Greek and Roman.

If you look at a map of ancient Greece, you can trace Theseus's journey to Athens. The cities and countries told about in the story were real. Theseus's journey wasn't really very long—only about 100 miles. If he had decided to sail to Athens instead of walking, he would have had to go only about 25 miles. But he wouldn't have had nearly as good a time. And he wouldn't have had as many chances to be a hero.

The story of how Theseus went to Athens is only the beginning. There are many other stories about Theseus's adventures. And each is just as exciting as this one.

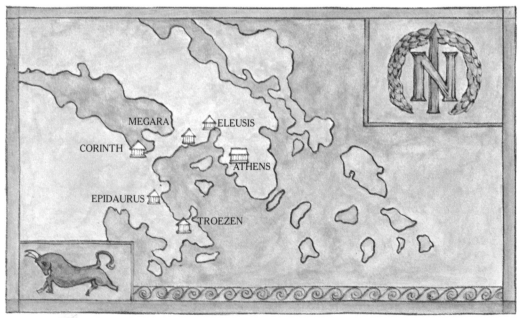

The road to Athens

King Aegeus ruled over the city of Athens. He was a rich and powerful king. But he was not happy. He was sad because he didn't have any children. "Who will take care of Athens when I die?" he wondered.

One day he heard that an old friend of his, King Pittheus, had a beautiful daughter named Aethra. Aegeus decided to pay his friend a visit. King Pittheus ruled over a city called Troezen, which was across the sea from Athens. So King Aegeus sailed to Troezen. As soon as he saw Aethra, he fell in love with her. Not long after, they were married.

When Aethra had a baby, King Aegeus was finally happy. He held his tiny son in his arms and smiled. "We will call him Theseus," he said. Then he turned to Aethra. "I must go back to Athens now," he told her. "But I want you and Theseus to stay here. There are some bad people in Athens. They want to take over the city when I die. If they knew I had a son, they would try to kill him."

Of course Aethra wanted to go to Athens with her husband. But she knew their baby would be in danger there. So she agreed to stay in Troezen and take care of Theseus.

The next morning King Aegeus took Aethra down to the shore. His ship was waiting there.

"If Theseus is going to rule Athens someday, he will have to be very strong," the king said. "So I'm going to make up a test for him."

The king dug a hole in the ground. He took off his sandals and his sword and put them into the hole. Then he covered the hole with a heavy stone.

"When you think Theseus is old enough and strong enough, bring him here," the king said. "If he is able to move the stone, tell him to put on my sword and sandals and bring them to me in Athens."

Then King Aegeus got on his ship and sailed away.

Theseus grew up to be a big, strong boy. He was very handsome and very smart. And he knew exactly what he wanted to be when he grew up. He wanted to be a famous hero like his cousin Heracles.

Once, when Theseus was only seven years old, Heracles came to visit King Pittheus. Heracles was wearing a lion's skin for a coat, but he took it off at dinner time. When the other boys saw the lion's skin on the ground, they were afraid and ran away. But Theseus picked up a little sword and ran right up to it. He wasn't afraid at all.

"Ho, ho!" laughed Heracles. "This little fellow is quite a hero!"

Then he reached down and mussed up Theseus's hair. Theseus never forgot that.

"I'm going to be as famous as Heracles someday," he promised his mother.

Aethra just smiled.

The years went by. Aethra watched her little boy become a young man. Finally she couldn't put it off any longer. "It's time for you to meet your father," she told Theseus. "But first there is something you must do."

Aethra took Theseus to the shore and pointed to the stone. "Your father, King Aegeus, left his sword and his sandals under that stone. If you can get them, you may go to Athens."

Theseus rolled the stone away in no time. He picked up the sandals and put them on his feet. He picked up the sword and strapped it to his belt.

"Now I am ready," he said.

When King Pittheus heard what had happened, he was very happy. "I will give you a ship so you can sail to Athens," he told Theseus.

"I don't want a ship," Theseus answered. "I want to walk."

"But the road to Athens is very dangerous!" King Pittheus cried. "It is full of robbers and bad men!"

"That's why I want to walk," Theseus said. "How am I ever going to be a hero if I do things the easy way?"

So Theseus started out. And it wasn't long before he had his first chance to be a hero. He was walking beside a dark forest in the land of Epidaurus, humming to himself and swinging his father's sword. All at once a man jumped out of the woods. It was the robber Periphetes. People called him "Club-Carrier" because he always carried a huge stick made of iron.

"I'm going to smash you!" Periphetes yelled at Theseus. "Just like I smash everyone who dares to walk on my road!"

"I'm glad to see you," Theseus answered. "I need a club like yours."

Then he killed Periphetes and took away his club.

When Theseus reached the land of Corinth, he met another bad man. This one was named Sinis. He was called "Tree-Bender" because he liked to bend trees down to the ground. Then he tied people to them. When he let the trees go, the people were torn to pieces.

"I'm going to kill you!" Sinis yelled at Theseus. "Just like I kill everyone who dares to walk on my road!"

"Oh, no, you're not," Theseus answered.

Before Sinis knew what was happening, he was tied to two trees that Theseus had bent down to the ground.

"It's only fair, after all," Theseus said. Then he let the trees go.

"Being a hero isn't so hard after all," Theseus said to himself. "I'm just getting started, and already I have gotten rid of two bad men."

But bad men weren't the only dangers on the road. The very next day Theseus killed a huge boar with sharp tusks. The boar liked to eat farmers and small children, so many people were glad when they heard what Theseus had done.

Theseus was having a wonderful time. He was feeling especially good on the day he met Sciron. Sciron lived on a cliff by the sea near the city of Megara. The road to Athens wound along the top of the cliff. Sciron stopped people who walked on the road. He forced them to wash his feet. Then, while they were busy trying to get his feet clean, Sciron kicked them over the cliff. There was a giant turtle living in the sea who ate the people Sciron kicked down to it.

"Hey, you!" Sciron hollered when he saw Theseus coming. "Before you can go any further, you have to wash my feet! Just like everyone who dares to walk on my road!"

But Theseus knew all about Sciron and his tricks. It wasn't long before the turtle was having Sciron for dinner.

"This is certainly a busy road!" Theseus said to himself. "I wonder who will come along next?"

As soon as he reached the land of Eleusis, he found out. There he met a wicked man named Cercyon. Cercyon liked to force people to wrestle with him. When they lost, which they always did, Cercyon killed them.

"Come and wrestle with me!" Cercyon shouted when
he saw Theseus. "Just like everyone who dares to walk
on my road!"

But Theseus was very strong. He threw Cercyon to
the ground, and then he killed him.

Now there was only one bad man left on the road to Athens. His name was Damastes. Damastes lived in a house by the side of the road. He pretended to be nice to travelers. He invited them into his house and gave them food. Then he asked them to spend the night.

Damastes had two beds. One was short and one was long. If someone wasn't tall enough for the long bed, Damastes tied him to it anyway. Then he pounded the person with a hammer and stretched him. If someone was too tall for the short bed, Damastes tied him to it anyway. Then he cut off the person's legs. Damastes had killed a lot of people by trying to make them fit into his beds.

When Damastes saw Theseus coming, he walked out into the road to greet him.

"Hello there!" Damastes said, smiling. "You must be tired and hungry. Why don't you come inside and have a bite to eat? Then you can spend the night in one of my nice beds. Just like everyone who walks on my road!"

But Theseus knew all about Damastes and his tricks. It wasn't long before Damastes was tied to his own short bed.

"You are just the right size for this bed," Theseus said. "But I'm going to cut off your head anyway. Then you won't bother any more travelers."

So Theseus killed Damastes too.

By now Athens was in sight. Theseus was very happy.

"My cousin Heracles once did twelve brave things in a row," he said to himself. "I have only done six, but I'm still young!"

Theseus's troubles weren't over yet, though. A mean witch named Medea lived in King Aegeus's palace. One day when Medea was doing some black magic, she found out that Theseus was on the road to Athens.

"Well, well!" she said, smiling wickedly. "I knew this would happen someday. That stupid King Aegeus thinks his son is a big secret. But I've known about him ever since he was born."

Then Medea frowned. "King Aegeus does whatever I tell him to do, and Theseus won't like that. I had better get rid of him soon." She pulled a dark cloud over her head and started thinking.

As soon as Theseus walked into the palace, Medea went to the king.

"Do you see that young man over there?" she whispered. "I have heard that he wants to kill you so he can rule Athens. Whatever you do, don't let him get near you!"

So King Aegeus refused to talk to Theseus. When it was time for dinner, he made Theseus sit all by himself at the end of the long, crowded table. Then he filled a wine cup with poison that Medea had made. He told one of his servants to give it to Theseus.

"Drink up!" the king shouted, raising his own wine cup. Everyone was supposed to drink along with the king.

But something was bothering Theseus. He was still wearing his father's sword, and it was sticking him in the side. So he decided to take the sword off before he drank his wine. He undid the straps and laid the sword on the table. Then he reached for his wine cup.

"WAIT!" King Aegeus shouted. He had seen the sword! And he knew that his son Theseus had come at last!

Medea got out of Athens in a hurry. She said a spell over herself and disappeared in a puff of smoke, right in front of everyone.

Meanwhile King Aegeus brought Theseus a new cup of wine. This one didn't have any poison in it. Then all the people at the table raised their cups and cheered.

Later, after everyone else had gone home, King Aegeus
and Theseus sat up talking. The light from the fireplace
flickered on the walls of the great hall. King Aegeus
wanted to hear all about his son's journey. And, because
Theseus didn't want to leave anything out of his story, the
two men sat there all night long.

PRONUNCIATION GUIDE

Aegeus: EE-jee-us
Aethra: EETH-ruh
Athens: ATH-enz
Cercyon: SUR-see-on
Corinth: KOR-inth
Damastes: duh-MASS-teez
Demeter: de-MEE-ter
Eleusis: eh-LOO-sis
Epidaurus: ep-ih-DOR-us
Heracles: HAIR-uh-kleez
Medea: mee-DEE-uh
Megara: MEG-ah-ruh
Periphetes: pair-ih-FEE-teez
Pittheus: PITH-ee-us
Poseidon: poe-SIE-dun
Sciron: SIE-ron
Sinis: SIE-niss
Theseus: THEE-see-us
Troezen: TREE-zen